## How to use this book

*Follow the advice, in italics, given for you on each page.*
*Support the children as they read the text that is shaded in cream.*
***Praise** the children at every step!*

*Detailed guidance is provided in the Read Write Inc. Phonics Handbook*

## 9 reading activities

*Children:*
*Practise reading the speed sounds.*
*Read the green, red and challenge words for the story.*
*Listen as you read the introduction.*
*Discuss the vocabulary check with you.*
*Read the story.*
*Re-read the story and discuss the 'questions to talk about'.*
*Read the story with fluency and expression.*
*Answer the questions to 'read and answer'.*
*Practise reading the speed words.*

# Speed sounds

## Consonants *Say the pure sounds (do not add 'uh').*

| f<br>ff<br>ph | l<br>ll<br>le | m<br>mm<br>**mb** | n<br>nn<br>kn | r<br>rr<br>wr | s<br>ss<br>se<br>**c**<br>**ce** | v<br>ve | z<br>zz<br>s | sh | th | ng<br>nk |
|---|---|---|---|---|---|---|---|---|---|---|

| b<br>bb | c<br>k<br>ck | d<br>dd | g<br>gg | h | j<br>g<br>**ge** | p<br>pp | qu | t<br>tt | w<br>wh | x | y | ch<br>tch |
|---|---|---|---|---|---|---|---|---|---|---|---|---|

## Vowels *Say the sounds in and out of order.*

| at | hen<br>head | in | on | up | day<br>make | see<br>tea<br>happy | high<br>smile<br>lie<br>find | blow<br>home<br>no |
|---|---|---|---|---|---|---|---|---|

| zoo<br>brute<br>blue | look | car | for<br>door<br>snore<br>yawn | fair<br>care | whirl<br>nurse<br>letter | shout<br>cow | boy<br>spoil |
|---|---|---|---|---|---|---|---|



*Each box contains one sound but sometimes more than one grapheme. Focus graphemes are **circled**.*

## Green words

*Read in Fred Talk (pure sounds).*

point reach round face hole time space noise huge

paw climb stair hair

spare square dare bare care share Clare

*Read in syllables.*

no\`tice trum\`pet

re\`pair soft\`ware fan\`fare com\`pare be\`ware pre\`pare

*Read the root word first and then with the ending.*

| | | | | | | | | |
|---|---|---|---|---|---|---|---|---|
| bore | → | bored | shout | → | shouted | reply | → | replied |
| make | → | making | scare | → | scared | glare | → | glared |
| declare | → | declared | stare | → | stared | flare | → | flared |

## Red words

two there who were you said your one

could what was school

## Challenge words

eyes reply

# I dare you

***Introduction***

*Have you ever played 'dare' games? What would you dare me to do? Have you ever started a good game and then it's 'gone too far'? What happened?*

*Radar Rob and Cosmic Clare are spacekids. They live on Planet Zox and they often get bored. One day they decide to play 'I dare you'. The tasks they dare each other are very different from the dares that Earth kids would do.*

*But, just like on Earth, sometimes it goes too far!*

Story written by Gill Munton
Illustrated by Tim Archbold

# Vocabulary check

Discuss the meaning (as used in the story) after the children have read each word.

| | definition: | sentence/phrase: |
|---|---|---|
| **prepare** | *get ready* | *Prepare to be very, very scared.* |
| **sprinted** | *ran fast* | *She peeled off her green skin, and sprinted off.* |
| **compare** | *decide what is the same between two things* | *"You can't compare that with running round the astroschool bare!"* |
| **chicken** | *coward* | *"Chicken!"shouted Clare.* |
| **declared** | *said, promised* | *"I'll get you back for that, Clare!" declared Rob.* |
| **crater** | *hole in the ground* | *She pointed to a small crater with a notice pinned to the rim.* |

***Punctuation to note in this story:***

1. *Capital letters to start sentences and full stops to end sentences*
2. *Capital letters for names*
3. *Exclamation marks to show anger, shock and surprise*
4. *'Wait and see' dots...*
5. *Speech marks*

## I dare you

There's a lot of spare time in space,
and the kids who live up there often get bored.

Like the time on Planet Zox when Radar Rob
(square blue body, six yellow legs, pointed head)
and Cosmic Clare (small, green, round)
were kicking a spaceball on the stairs
before astroschool one day ...

"Let's play 'I dare you'," said Clare.
"You start."

"Okay," said Rob.
"Prepare to be very, very scared, Clare.
I dare you to ...

... peel off your green skin,
and run round the astroschool – bare!"

"I'm not scared!" said Clare.
She peeled off her green skin, and sprinted off.

"I've got a good one for you, Rob," said Clare as she stepped back into her skin.

"I dare you to ...

... put on a pair of moonboots – no, you'll need three pairs, Rob – and climb to the top of the radar mast!"

"That's not fair!" said Rob.

He glared at Clare.

"You can't compare that with running round the astroschool bare!"

"Chicken!" shouted Clare. So off Rob went.

"I'll get you back for that, Clare!" declared Rob.

I dare you to …

stand on a chair and play a fanfare

on your rocket-boosted trumpet,

throwing your space hat in the air at the same time."

Clare stared at him.

"You look a bit green, Clare," said Rob.

"I always do!" Clare replied, reaching for her trumpet.

"You're not going to like this one, Rob," said Clare.

"I dare you to ...

... go in there!"

She pointed to a small crater with a notice pinned to the rim.

The notice said, "Beware of the robodog!"

Two huge hairy paws rested on the rim of the crater.

Two bulging yellow eyes glared at Rob. Two red nostrils flared.

"Take care!" said Clare.

Clare couldn't see what happened next. But there was a lot of noise.

"Woof!" "Crash!" "Clank!" "Woof-woof!" "Boff!" "Help!"

Then Rob's pointed face (fairly red) peeped out of the crater, followed by his six yellow legs (a bit bent).

There was a big hole in his square body, and his chest was making a ticking sound.

"Are you all right?" asked Clare.

"No, I'm not!

I'll have to reprogram all my software!"

said Rob, reaching inside his chest.

"I'll help to repair you," said Clare.

"And you can share my Star Bar if you like."

"Okay," said Rob.

"That seems fair. Just one more thing – no more games of 'I dare you'!"

# Questions to talk about

*Re-read the page. Read the question to the children. Tell them whether it is a* **FIND IT** *question or* **PROVE IT** *question.*

| FIND IT | PROVE IT |
|---|---|
| ✓ *Turn to the page* | ✓ *Turn to the page* |
| ✓ *Read the question* | ✓ *Read the question* |
| ✓ *Find the answer* | ✓ *Find your evidence* |
| | ✓ *Explain why* |

| | | |
|---|---|---|
| **Page 9:** | FIND IT | *Why do kids often get bored on Planet Zox?* |
| **Page 10:** | FIND IT | *What does Rob dare Clare to do?* |
| **Page 11:** | PROVE IT | *Why does Rob complain about his dare?*<br>*Which dare would you rather do? Why?* |
| **Page 12:** | PROVE IT | *What does Rob mean when he says "You look a bit green"?* |
| **Page 13:** | PROVE IT | *Would you carry out Clare's dare?* |
| **Page 14:** | PROVE IT | *What happened to Rob in the crater?* |
| **Page 15:** | PROVE IT | *How does Clare try to make things better for Rob?*<br>*Why do they agree not to play the game any more?* |

# Questions to read and answer

*(Children complete without your help.)*

1. Why can it be boring in space?

2. What is Rob's first dare to Clare?

3. Why does Rob say Clare's dare is not fair?

4. What does the robodog look like?

5. Why do you think giving dares is not a good thing?

# Speed words

*Children practise reading the words across the rows, down the columns and in and out of order clearly and quickly.*

| | | | | |
|---|---|---|---|---|
| face | huge | bored | yellow | shouted |
| reaching | spare | bare | beware | declared |
| glared | scared | two | could | were |
| many | doesn't | watch | someone | how |